ANNO'S DENMARK

by

Mitsumasa Anno

ANNO'S JOURNEY VI by Mitsumasa Anno
Illustrations © Kuso-kobo 2004
Originally published by Fukuinkan Shoten Publishers, Inc., Tokyo, Japan, in 2004
under the title of "TABI NO EHON VI"
The English language rights arranged with Fukuinkan Shoten Publishers, Inc., Tokyo
All rights reserved.
© Copyright 2018
Beautiful Feet Books, Inc.
San Luis Obispo, CA 93401
www.bfbooks.com
All rights reserved. No part of this publication may be reproduced in any
form without written permission from the publisher.
English translation by Miki Kobayashi, edited by Rea Berg © 2018
ISBN: 978-1-893103-75-7 (pbk.)
978-1-893103-76-4 (HB)
Library of Congress Control Number: 2018941532
Printed in the United States of America
First American Edition

Anno's Denmark

My first trip to Europe was about forty years ago. The city I visited first was Copenhagen. It was veiled in mist, and I felt as if I was in a world of fairy tales. I also visited Odense, where I stayed at a cheap hotel in front of a station. I made friends with a boy in the street and showed him my paintings of tin soldiers, eleven swans, and the naked emperor. He must have understood something and led me to the Hans Christian Andersen Museum. It was not so grand as it is now, but I felt a strong affinity with the visitors from all over the world, who were connected by Andersen.

The first *Andersen's Fairy Tales* I heard were "The Tinderbox" and "Little Claus and Big Claus," read by our teacher when I was in fifth grade. I was so charmed with the tales that I borrowed a copy of *Andersen's Fairy Tales* myself. I had never read such an absurd and interesting story as "Little Claus and Big Claus." Afterward, I read Andersen's novel, *The Improvisatore*, translated into Japanese. It is a book I will take with me if I am spending my holidays on a desert island.

I visited Andersen's birthplace in Denmark many times. When I said I would like to include Denmark in my *Anno's Journey* series, a certain person worried if such a small country could offer enough worthy scenes. I wasn't worried at all; if I illustrated all the *Andersen's Fairy Tales*, I thought, the book would soon be filled. In fact, I omitted some of the tales, which were difficult to illustrate because of the plots or settings and which seemed to be out of date. However, I hope that you, even if you are not familiar with *Andersen's Fairy Tales*, will enjoy finding the scenes from the world of Andersen's imagination.

The trip from the capital city, Copenhagen, which is on an island, to Odense is by sea. In old times, if you took an appointed train at Copenhagen, it was loaded on a ship crossing the sea to Odense and carried you there even if you were sleeping on the train. Nowadays a long, long bridge has been built from Copenhagen to Odense; trains and vehicles can easily come and go between the cities using the bridge.

Denmark is a small country, but there are many things to be learned from its people, who are proud of their country and its green woods and pastures. Andersen was born in 1805 and died in 1875. The year 2005 marked the 200th anniversary of his birth.

August 2, 2004
Mitsumasa Anno

Cover

In Denmark, there is a game in which a player pierces a ring with a spear while riding horseback.

Frontispiece

This is the neighborhood of the Hans Christian Andersen Museum in Odense.

Scene 1

Each scene is a landscape of Denmark, in which I depicted events and characters from *Andersen's Fairy Tales*. Here, I will introduce brief synopses of the illustrated tales.

The northernmost town in Denmark is Skagen. The northern tip of Skagen is a sandbar popular with tourists, who arrive by coaches. In this scene, I have included pictures from two tales—"The Conceited Apple-Branch" and "The Top And Ball." In the first tale, apple blossoms are praised for their beauty and loved by everyone. They despise dandelions, which are called "Devil's Milk Pails" and ignored because they are humdrum. However, all the flowers are dear to the sun. The tale of "The Top and Ball" is about the dangers of thinking too highly of oneself.

Scene 2

In Skagen, the sea often gets rough and dark in winter. In old days, they used a bonfire called Skagen's Vippefyr—firewood burned in a basket and hoisted in the air on a fulcrum, twenty-five meters above the ground. The light this cast was for boats offshore to know where a harbor was. Another method of hoisting a beacon was done using kites. In Scene 14, at the lower left, you will see two people flying a kite with a lantern.

In Andersen's "The Windmill," the mill laments, "I always have to have a stone mill in my chest, wings on my head and a balcony around my waist. Some people might say such a thing is putting on airs, but I am just doing my job."

Scene 3

At the mouth of the Baltic Sea, 180 kilometers offshore from the main island, is Bornholm. The island is famous for the ruins of Hammershus. Depicted here is a scene after a circus show has ended. Both the circus company and the travelers cannot go out of this page, in reality, but . . .

Scene 4

. . . Let them move on to this illustration featuring a white circular church.

In Andersen's "The Fir Tree," the small fir tree is never content and always thinks happiness will be in his future. I often came across vast fir forests in the countryside of Denmark.

In "Two Maidens," the name "maiden" refers to a tool used to ram down the paving stones in the roads. But the two maidens in this story refuse to have their names changed.

In "The Beetle Who Went on His Travels," a vainglorious beetle asks a blacksmith to make him a pair of golden shoes that he believes will make him as respectable as the king's horse, but in vain. However, after many humiliating adventures on his travels, the beetle returns home as conceited as ever.

Scene 5

"The Ugly Duckling" is a tale you will surely know.

In "The Swineherd," a prince of a small kingdom wants to marry a princess of an emperor. He manages to get a job as a swineherd in the emperor's castle. In his free time, he makes a pot with little bells around the rim. The pot rings so nicely that the princess, who happens to hear the sound, wishes for it at any cost.

In one of the scenes in *Anno's Journey* (the first of this series, depicting Central Europe) is a picture of a man who escapes from prison. I hear that some people assume the escaped prisoner must be hiding somewhere and search all the pages. To meet their expectation, I painted a picture of the prisoner in *Anno's Italy*. However, it was not so satisfactory to me, so I let him appear again in this scene. Enjoy finding out where he runs.

Scene 6

The model of this illustration is Odense, Andersen's birthplace and the location of the Hans Christian Andersen Museum. At the right is St. Canute's Cathedral, where Hans received Confirmation at age fourteen. I illustrated children who have just finished the ceremony. In "The Red Shoes," a little girl named Karen is given a pair of red shoes and is happy wearing the shoes, until the day a frightening angel appears to her and says, "You shall dance in your red shoes until you are pale and cold!"

In "The Old Street Lamp," an old lamp must be retired after long service and be parted from the watchman and his wife, who faithfully supply it with oil every day. What will happen to it once it resigns? It may be sent to an iron foundry and made into something different. The watchman decides to beg for the lamp and keep it in his house.

"The Bell-Deep" is a story about a bell that tolls in the deep pool of a river in the town of Odense. The bell hangs in the church tower observing many things. One day, the bell breaks loose and flies down into the deepest part of the river. It continues to ring, telling stories to a lonely old river spirit.

"Under The Willow Tree" is my favorite tale, the sad story of a boy and a girl—Knud and Joanna—who grow up together in a small town. Knud becomes a journeyman shoemaker in Copenhagen, where Joanna is a professional singer. Knud has loved Joanna since childhood and wants to marry her, but their relationship has not developed as he had hoped. At the lower right, Knud is going on a journey, waving his hand.

In the tale "The Storks," Andersen has incorporated the folk belief that storks deliver babies to families. Real storks come to Denmark too, all the way from Africa, and build nests on chimneys or utility poles.

SCENE 7

The model of this illustration is Ribe, a city famous for night watchmen.

"The Emperor's New Suit" is a story about a gullible but naked emperor, who wears "a splendid suit of cloth fools cannot see" and shows it off. His story begins in this scene. Look for the ending and what happens to the swindlers.

In the tale "Stupid Hans," three brothers hear that the youth who can tell the most wonderful tale should marry a princess. The elder brothers are smart and learned, so they confidently ride their horses to the castle. The unwitting younger brother, Hans, follows his brothers, riding a goat. When the elder brothers arrive, they get nervous in front of the princess and cannot speak. On the other hand, Hans, instead of telling a tale, acts wildly and presents the princess a crow carcass he picked up on the way and recklessly throws dirt at secretaries in the castle. The amazed princess says, "How wonderful you are! You did something I never could!" and incredibly, she decides to marry him.

"The Elf of the Rose" is a story about lovers told by a rose-elf, and "The Little Match Seller" is too famous to need explanation. In "She Was Good For Nothing," a poor washerwoman washes clothes in the river, but the water is so cold she asks her son to bring a bottle of wine to warm her. When she was young, she served the counselor and fell in love with his son but was not allowed to marry him and was obliged to marry a glovemaker, named Eric. Soon they have a son, but Eric becomes ill and dies. She suffers a lot, working as laundress and raising her son alone, and in the end, dies while working in the water. Although she is sometimes told, "She is good for nothing," she is working hard. A bottle of wine is just to warm her.

"Ole-Luk-Oie—The Dream-God" comes to children each night as they fall asleep and relates wonderful stories. Because he is invisible, the children feel as if they had visited a fantasy world listening to the stories. In *Andersen's Fairy Tales*, there are seven stories Ole-Luk-Oie tells a little boy named Hjalmar.

"The Jumper" is a story of a flea, a grasshopper, and a skipjack, who hold a jumping competition. Who do you think will jump the highest and win the hand of the princess?

In "Little Ida's Flowers," Ida has a friend, a student who is good at storytelling and paper cutting, like Andersen himself. When Ida asks why her favorite flowers are withered, her friend tells her the flowers were at a castle ball the previous night and got quite tired. She is charmed with the story and hopes to see the pretty flowers dancing.

In "Little Tiny or Thumbelina," a woman is given a seed by a fairy that she plants in a flower pot. The seed grows into a beautiful tulip, within which sits a very delicate girl as tiny as a thumb. A toad and a mole both want to marry her, which causes her a lot of trouble.

In "The Bottle Neck," the broken neck of an old wine bottle laments its former glory days when its cork was drawn to celebrate the joyous betrothal of a lovely girl and a young sailor. The bottleneck reminisces upon how it came to hang in the window of a poor house where it is used to hold water in a bent old birdcage.

In the tale "The Angel," whenever a child dies, an angel comes down from heaven, picks up the dead child, and carries him to the places the child has loved and gathers handfuls of flowers to bring to heaven. Before they reach heaven, the angel sees a withered field flower and says they must also take it with them. The angel tells the moving story of why the dead flower is so important.

At a feast held by a mouse-king, "Soup from a Sausage Skewer" becomes a topic of conversation. The mouse-king declares that the young lady mouse who can cook the best soup shall be his queen. What a fine offer! Four young female mice set out on a journey to learn how to make skewer soup.

Scene 8

In the tale "The Little Green Ones," a healthy young rose tree becomes ill when an army of tiny soldiers in green uniforms attacks it. These green soldiers are great friends with the ants, though human beings detest them and try to kill them with soapsuds. What are the little soldiers? At the lower right, I depicted rose bushes.

A delightful tale that I'll never forget is "Little Claus and Big Claus," in which Little Claus defeats Big Claus, who is always hard on him. In my childhood, I got excited everytime I read the story. The first part of the story is depicted here, and the conclusion is in Scene 10.

In "The Princess and the Pea," a pea is laid on the bottom of a bed stand, with twenty mattresses on top of the pea, and another twenty eiderdown beds on top of that. The test of a real princess is whether she can feel the pea through all those layers.

In "The Porter's Son," a former general lives on the first floor; his porter lives in the cellar. The general has a baby daughter named Emily; the porter has a bright little boy named George, who is very good at amusing Emily. But the great difference in rank between the two families means George must study hard to be approved by the general and his wife. Fortunately, George has a brilliant mind and works diligently to better himself.

In "The Boots Of Happiness," two fairies are talking, and the younger one says, "I was given a pair of boots today and told to bring them to the world of mortals. Whoever wears the boots will be transported to a place or a time period the person longs for the most. Thus, every mortal will be happy. . . ." But the elder fairy says, "Far from being happy, they will become unhappy." A Councilor, named Knap, happens to put on the boots, as does a night watchman, and then a hospital assistant. In each case, the magic boots do not bring the happiness they had hoped for.

Other scenes from *Andersen's Fairy Tales* depicted here include "The Snow Man," "Aunty Toothache," "The Little Match Girl," and "Thumbelina."

Scene 9

In the center is depicted a statue of a man with a whip, which I saw in Toender, a town that borders Germany. Although I didn't know who he was, the statue was colorful and amusing. On the left, you'll see a man turning the handle of a box near the gate. He is a local music box player. You'll find a carriage, a pottery, and men gathering reeds for roofing. Throughout Denmark, old buildings like those in this scene have been well-preserved and are still in use.

Scene 10

This scene is of Copenhagen, with the Stork Fountain at the right and in the center a statue of "musicians playing old musical instruments" by Siegfried Wagner. Under the tower, you'll see a statue of Andersen, which stands near the Tivoli Gardens. At the lower right is the city hall of Copenhagen. You-know-who is marching on the main road, and his two swindlers are explaining frantically on the right and running away on the left. On the bridge at the upper left are Big Claus and Little Claus.

Scene 11

From here, in four scenes, I'll guide you around the famous Tivoli Gardens, an amusement park both adults and children enjoy.

In "The Races," the time has come when prizes are awarded for the swiftest runner of the year. A hare wins the first prize and a snail the second, after a lively discussion between a swallow, a fly, and a wild rose.

In "The Nightingale," visitors to China hear the song of a small bird called a nightingale and admire its beauty; some of them write about the bird in their books. It is not until the Chinese emperor reads those books that he learns of the bird. He orders his people to find the bird and bring it to him. He is amazed at its marvelous voice and treats it with loving care. One day, a parcel is delivered to him; inside is a bejeweled but artificial nightingale that can sing wonderfully. As the emperor pays more attention to the artificial bird, the real nightingale flies away to her own woods. What do you think happens to the emperor in the end?

In "What The Old Man Does Is Always Right," an old peasant rides his horse to a fair. On the way, he exchanges the horse for a cow and later the cow for a sheep. Although he continuously trades for items of less and less value, his wife believes what he does is always right.

A child riding a reindeer is an inspiration from "The Snow Queen." In this tale, a demon has a magic looking-glass which makes everything beautiful look ugly and everything bad look even worse. One day the demon's pupils try to fly high, holding the mirror to see the angels and gods, but they carelessly let it fall to the earth. It breaks into pieces and scatters all over the world where the fragments, which have the same power as the whole mirror, can fly into a person's eye. This is what happens to a boy named Kai and a girl named Gerda, who had been good friends until Kai is struck by a fragment and suddenly becomes spiteful. In the meantime, the Snow Queen appears, takes Kai away and flies over the black clouds. Kai forgets Gerda completely, while Gerda is so worried about Kai that she decides to search for him by herself. On the way, she is troubled by an old witch, a strange palace, and robbers. However, a little robber girl feels pity for Gerda and asks a reindeer to take her to Lapland, on the edge of the North; the Snow Queen's castle is supposed to be there. Gerda rides on the reindeer and leaves for Lapland. Can she really find Kai there?

Scene 12

This is a haunted area in the Tivoli Gardens with lots of ghostly things. *Andersen's Fairy Tales* has a variety of mysterious stories, including "The Old Grave-Stone," which concerns a weathered gravestone in the courtyard of a house, on which the children like to play. Though the names are barely visible, when one of the children deciphers two names, an old man tells the tale of the couple featured, and the esteem and respect this couple had enjoyed in the community. He had heard their story as a young boy, and here retells it.

"The Child In The Grave" tells the tale of the youngest child of a family who dies and is buried. The mother grieves over her only son so much that she forgets the living and follows Death down into an underground hall where her dead child dwells. She has a heavenly encounter with her son, which restores her faith and enables her to return with joy to her husband and daughters.

In "The Elfin Hill," a great ball is to be held on an elfin hill, and various creatures like elves, a merman, a night raven and will-o'-the-wisps gather. Who is the important guest the elfin king and his seven daughters are waiting for?

In "The Toad," a toad family dwells deep in a well. One day, the smallest toad jumps into a bucket about to be drawn up and goes out into the world. What does she see there?

"The Girl Who Trod On The Loaf" is about a girl named Inge who is beautiful but cruel. She is taken into the service of wealthy people. After one year passes, she is told to visit her parents. She dresses in new finery and sets out. Coming across the moor in the way, she puts a large loaf of bread given by her mistress into the mud, and steps on it so as not to wet her feet. But the loaf starts to sink under her and she is drowned. At the bottom of the marsh lives the Marsh Woman who takes Inge into her service.

The tale of "The Old House" presents a very old house, which is almost in ruins and disliked in the whole neighborhood. A solitary old man lives there, and one day a little boy from the house opposite makes friends with him. Eventually, the old man dies, and the old house is torn down and a new one built. The little boy grows up to be a good man, gets married, and moves to that very house. One day his wife finds a tin soldier in the soil of the garden. It is the one the little boy gave to the old man as a gift.

An owner of a puppet show wishes life was breathed into his puppets so that they would perform as he commands. In "The Puppet-Show Man" his dream comes true, but his animated puppets are far more difficult to handle.

A soldier in "The Tinderbox" is told by a witch to go down into a hollow tree, get through some chambers guarded by dogs, and fetch a tinderbox, which turns out to be a magical one.

A beetle is depicted again in this scene. Can you find it?

Scene 13

Here, I have illustrated another scene from "The Conceited Apple-Branch."

"Little Tuck" is about a boy named Charles, though everyone calls him Tuck. One day, he helps an old washerwoman carry a pail of water, and that night she makes him dream a wonderful dream. In the dream, he gallops on horseback with a knight, meets a sailor, and talks with a peasant woman. He also dreams of his little sister who has grown up to be a beautiful young girl. But when he wakes up, he remembers nothing of his dream.

The protagonist in "The Flying Trunk" inherits his dead father's wealth, lives a luxurious life, and soon uses up all his riches. Then one of his friends sends him a trunk. Having nothing to pack, he climbs into the trunk, and then . . . the trunk flies high into the sky and arrives at the distant land of Turkey. What's waiting for him?

In "The Comet," an old man remembers seeing Halley's Comet when he was very young, and now as the comet returns, he reminisces about all the events of his life.

Isaac Newton stated that comets move under the law of gravitation. Edmund Halley calculated the past observation data and concluded that the comet that appeared in 1531, 1607, and 1682 was the same one returning about every 76 years. He further predicted the comet would be visible in 1758 or early in 1759. His prediction proved to be correct through the observation of the comet by Johann Georg Palitzsch, a German amateur astronomer. Most recently, the Halley comet appeared in 1986; its previous appearance was in 1910. So it must have appeared when Andersen, born in 1805, was about thirty years old.

"Ole the Tower-Keeper" wishes for a solitary life and becomes a keeper of a church tower. He spends most of his time reading. Among the books he reads is a book on geology, including an explanation about boulders. He is so engaged in the book that he forgets his favorite New Year's event, namely to watch all the struggling poets, musicians, and newspaper writers, flying on their writing quills to Amager.

Scene 14

Here is the exit from the Tivoli Gardens. At the upper right is the Gefion Fountain, based on Norse mythology. This is what it says: One day, the Swedish king Gylfe told the goddess Gefion that he would offer as much land as she was able to plough within one day and one night. Therefore, she transformed her four sons into oxen, had them plough, and created Zealand.

In the four following tales, objects and real things argue as to their value. In "The Pen and the Inkstand," the pen and the inkstand dispute who is the real storyteller. The inkstand remarks that all the poet's works come out of it and a pen is just writing the words down. Then, the pen insists that it does narrate and write, while the inkstand is just supplying the means to write.

"The Money-Box" is shaped like a pig, something we call a "piggy bank." In this tale, the piggy bank falls on the ground and breaks into pieces.

In "The Candles," a wax candle boasts of lighting up gorgeous ballrooms. On the other hand, a tallow candle is content with throwing light in the kitchen of a poor family. The tallow candle is content to see the beaming faces of the family illumined by its light.

"The Farm-Yard Cock and the Weathercock" presents an argument between a real cock and a weathervane. The yard cock rules over hens and chicks and acts like a lord. The weathercock on the roof observes birds flying in the sky. It thinks the world is boring and everything is very stupid. It breaks off as if it could not bear standing on the roof anymore.

In "The Pea Blossom," five peas in a shell are picked by a boy and shot through his peashooter. One of the peas is disappointed as it lands in the gutter of a poor garret. But this little pea changes the life of a poor and sickly young girl.

"The Little Mermaid" is set in a castle at the bottom of the sea where mermaid sisters dwell. The mermaids are allowed to surface and see the world above the sea when they are fifteen years old. When the youngest sister turns fifteen, she surfaces and falls in love with a handsome prince whose ship is at anchor. When a fierce storm arises, the vessel capsizes, and the prince nearly drowns, but the mermaid rescues him. Determined to be with the prince she loves, the mermaid knows she must forfeit her ability to speak, and so the prince never learns of her love for him or that she was the one who saved him.

At the left is the statue of the Little Mermaid at the harbor of Copenhagen, made by Edvard Eriksen in 1913.

Scene 15

The town of Nyhavn, in Copenhagen, was once an important inlet for ships transporting goods to the old inner city. It is now a tourist sight of Copenhagen. No vessels other than old ones are allowed to anchor there. Andersen lived in Nyhavn from 1845 to 1864, and there is a memorial plaque at his former address at No. 67.

"The Shepherdess and the Sweep" is the tale of a china shepherdess and a china chimney sweep that live in an ornate old cupboard. The china chimney sweep dares to escape from the cupboard by climbing up the chimney along with his sweetheart the china shepherdess and goes out into the wide world.

"The Brave Tin Soldier" has only one leg for lack of melted tin. He was a gift, along with his fellow soldiers, to a young boy for his birthday. The tin soldiers live with other playthings such as a jack-in-a-box or a nutcracker, and the soldier with one leg falls in love with a little dancer. Because the tiny dancer is always balancing on one leg, the soldier believes she has but one leg too. One day, the soldier falls out of the window into the street below, is put on a paper boat by mischievous boys, and sent sailing down a gutter. After a great deal of trouble, he returns to his dear love again.

Scene 16

This is a square in front of the palaces of Amalienborg. Here you can see the Changing of the Guard, a royal custom even if there are just two guards. When the monarch is in residence, the military band comes from Rosenborg Castle and marches alongside the Changing at noon.

Scene 17

In olden days, even large sailing vessels were made of wood. This is a dry dock for shipbuilding.

Scene 18

To the north of Copenhagen is a town called Helsingor (Elsinore). It is famous for the Castle Kronborg, which is the setting of William Shakespeare's *Hamlet* and thus a popular tourist spot. In the play, Hamlet suspects his father has been poisoned by his uncle, the newly crowned monarch, and reconstructs the scene on a stage in front of the new king and queen. The king gets very upset watching the crime he committed acted out as a drama.

Scene 19

This is the countryside of Denmark. In "The Story Of The Wind," the wind that blows through the hills and fields of Denmark has seen many things. The Wind tells the story of a rich man, called Waldemar Daa, and his wife and three daughters, who are as beautiful as a rose, a lily, and a hyacinth. Waldemar Daa is building a large ship and must fell many trees of the forest. In one of the trees, Anna Dorothea, the youngest daughter, finds a stork building her nest and asks her father not to cut down the tree.

Waldemar gets possessed with alchemy, the art of making gold, and for days experiments and concocts mixtures. Alchemy is a fantastic unattainable dream, but Waldemar Das cannot give it up and finally ruins himself because of it. He sells his mansion, and the family is broken up.

Many years pass, and Anna Dorothea is old and living in a miserable hut. It looks nearly collapsed but is secure thanks to the nest a stork has built on the roof.

In this scene, I depicted the end of "Under The Willow Tree," where Knud returns to his hometown and dies under a willow tree.

In "The Wicked Prince," an evil prince is set on the conquest of the world. He rules the conquered people by fear, devastating their countries by fire and the sword. Afterward, he brings all the wealth from these conquests to his castle. Finally, he tries to break the walls of heaven with his powerful ships. However, this time his arrogance has gone too far; and God sends a swarm of gnats.

SCENE 20

In the north of Denmark is a large city called Aalborg, and to the north of it there is a place called Lindholm Hoje, which is famous for the ruins of the Viking age. It used to be a burial ground of soldiers killed in battle.

In "The Wild Swans," eleven princes and their sister named Eliza are living happily. But one day, their beloved father, who is king, marries a wicked woman. The new mother sends Eliza to live with a peasant in the country, and then she transforms the eleven princes into swans. Eliza, now a beautiful young lady of fifteen, returns home, but soon leaves the castle to search for her missing brothers. In trying to help her brothers, she is mistaken for a witch and about to be executed. But her eagerness to save her brothers is far greater than the fear of death.

SCENE 21

In this last scene you'll see the Little Mermaid. To me, she seems not only a symbol of Hans Christian Andersen, but also of Denmark, and so I have depicted her here again.

ANNO MITSUMASA

A life is worth living just by reading books.
The child who doesn't read, will likely grow up to be a person who doesn't read in their lifetime.
—Mitsumasa Anno

When Mitsumasa Anno was in his late 30s, he fulfilled a lifelong dream to travel to Europe, beginning his adventure in the beautiful city of Copenhagen. Anno had loved the fairy tales of Hans Christian Andersen since a boy when his fifth-grade teacher first read "Little Claus and Big Claus" to his class. Arriving in fog-veiled Copenhagen seemed to Anno like a scene right out of those beloved tales.

Mitsumasa Anno was born in 1926 in Tsuwano, Japan—a small village surrounded by mountains. Anno recalls of his childhood, "On the other side of the mountains were villages with rice fields, and beyond these rice fields was the ocean, which seemed to be very, very far away… because my world was cut off from the outside world, first by the mountains and then by the ocean, the desire to go and see what lay on the other side grew stronger."

His European adventures resulted some years later in the first of his *Journey* series of books, titled *Anno's Journey*, published in 1977. Northern European pastoral and village scenes fill the pages of this book, revealing the author's love for the art, architecture, literature, and culture, of these historically rich lands. This book was followed by *Anno's Italy* (1979), *Anno's Britain* (1982), *Anno's USA* (1983), *Anno's Spain* (2004), and *Anno's Denmark* (2005). In 2009, *Anno's China* was published in Japan and introduced to an American audience in 2017.

One of the inspirations for *Anno's Denmark* was the 200th anniversary of Hans Christian Andersen's birth, celebrated in 2005; the book comprises a humble homage from one devoted artist to another. Mitsumasa Anno visited the museum of Hans Christian Andersen in Odense many times, and on one of his visits there, recalls a watershed moment he credits to Andersen. Studying Andersen's sketches, he was struck by, "finding them to be so much at ease, so unpretentious, and so un-self-conscious." Later he recalls

I hypnotized myself and said to myself that I was Hans Christian Andersen. I am not a professional artist so I can do anything when it comes to painting. That experience was a turning point in my life in the sense of pride in being an artist, which has restricted me so much, bound me so much; it was gone at the time. And since that time I have found so much pleasure in doing the work.

It is fitting that Mitsumasa Anno's work has been awarded the most prestigious honor in the world of children's books—The Hans Christian Andersen Award (1984). It is no surprise given the debt Anno felt to Andersen's influence on his art, that he would create such a work of joy, humor, and whimsy, as is evident here in *Anno's Denmark*. Beautiful Feet Books is honored to continue Mr. Anno's legacy by presenting the beauty of his art and thoughts to an English-speaking audience for the very first time.

—Rea Berg, Publisher